LUCY NEWLYN was born in Uganda and grew up in Leeds. She is now Professor of English Language and Literature at Oxford University, and a Fellow of St Edmund Hall. She has published widely on English Romantic literature, and is the editor of *The Cambridge Companion to Coleridge* (CUP, 2003). Her book *Reading, Writing and Romanticism: The Anxiety of Reception* (OUP, 2000) won the British Academy's Rose Mary Crawshay prize in 2001. She has co-edited *Synergies: Creative Writing in Academic Practice* (Holywell Press for St Edmund Hall, 2003, 2004). Married with a daughter and two step-children, she lives in Oxford, where she is working on the writings of Edward Thomas.

LUCY NEWLYN

Ginnel

Oxford*Poets*

CARCANET

First published in Great Britain in 2005 by
Carcanet Press Limited
Alliance House
Cross Street
Manchester M2 7AQ

A CIP catalogue record for this book is available from the British Library
ISBN 1 903039 74 6

The publisher acknowledges financial assistance from Arts Council England

Typeset by XL Publishing Services, Tiverton
Printed and bound in England by SRP Ltd, Exeter

for my mother
in memory of my father

Walter Tessier Newlyn
1915–2002

Acknowledgements

I could not have written these poems without the support and encouragement of David Constantine, Jenny Harrison, Hermione Lee, Jenny Lewis, Doreen Newlyn, Bernard O'Donoghue, Martin Slater and members of the St Edmund Hall Poetry Workshop (especially Ben, Lizzie and Caroline). I am also extremely fortunate to have had detailed feedback on early drafts of the sequence from Carmen Bugan, Justin Gosling, Jane Griffiths, and John Powell Ward. To all of these people I am deeply grateful.

Versions of 'Landscape near Otley' and 'Penny for the Guy' have been published in the *Oxford Magazine*. 'Playin' Out' was first published in *Keystone*.

Contents

Why go straight? There is nothing at the end of any road better than may be found beside it, though there would be no travel, did men believe it.

Edward Thomas, 'On roads and footpaths'

Ginnel

Gennel, ginnel Also *genn-ginn-gynnell, jennel. [Of obscure origin: sense
1 suggests that it may be a corruption of chenelle CHANNEL]*
1 = CHANNEL Obs.
2. *dial. A long narrow passage between houses, either roofed or unroofed.*
Oxford English Dictionary

You lost your French roots long ago:
came north, toughened your grain.
Liked it here, settled in;

never went south again –
never went further, if you could help it,
than the end of Yorkshire.

Was it the matt templates of grey,
the stone walls against grey sky,
light scarce and edging across cobbles?

Was it the way cloud massed on hills,
wind hammered fells,
bent bracken, rocked dry-stone walls?

Was it the houses huddled in the wind's grip,
wind raking the beck,
leaves driven in hordes against houses?

You thinned down, like an eel,
bending your body like a beck
between houses. You branched out,

sending fine veins toward the fells,
covering the land with cracks,
as a river crumples a map with fissures.

They'd not know you in middle England,
your looks are so altered.
The sun tips shadows over your high edges;

wind pelts you with detritus.
You are long and stony and grained.
Footfalls reverberate, lost in your still chambers.

Home

starts here, in the flange of a fan,
where three steep terraces, one by one,

climb away to the left, and Brookfield Road
drops sudden, down and round

(with a change of gear, or a pause
in the clip-clop cobbly sound)

and the world folds up to the nub
where a corner shop stands,

or opens out like the palm of a hand,
and Monkbridge Road curves on and on.

Two addresses

It never puzzled me as a child
that our house had two addresses.
The postman delivered to either side
and neighbours used both entrances.

At the front, on the Headingley side,
lay lawns and grey stone terraces.
Pavements were tidy, verges lined
with cherries and acacias.

Privet hedges, neat and trimly styled,
had flower beds along their bases,
and children played in gardens filled
with honeysuckle, jasmine, roses.

At the back, on the Meanwood side,
were narrow rows of red brick houses.
Washing hung looped between tiled
roofs like ragged necklaces.

Streets were cobbled, ginnels stiled,
kids hung about in parking places.
Smog blackened, dustbins spilled,
and shirt-sleeved men in yards wore braces.

Light

in the morning was new, quick;
picked out bird on sky, leaf on twig;
set shadows dancing on stone and brick.

At breakfast, our kitchen filled
with light: it streamed through windows, spilled
on tables – wouldn't be held or stilled.

It stole through the house like a lean cat,
touching this, leaving prints on that;
in the mornings, hunted – or sat

watching in curtains and hiding
in corners. Moving soundlessly,
gliding through doorways,

it gleamed in mirrors, played
on planes, was tempted and beguiled
by polished surfaces. Agile,

lithe, it spun in the air – crept
along floors; chased specks of dust; leapt
after motes and seldom slept.

In the afternoons, our kitchen was cool.
It held coolness, as a deep bowl
holds water. Darkness filled the hall.

But the lounge was a great pool of white:
sun drenching air, space flooding sight.
Free and indifferent, the wide bright light.

Washing day

That great white sheet on the line
is big-bellied with buffeting wind,
and the woman is pegging it
with hands bent on pummelling bread.

The big-bellied woman is beaten
by the wind, and blown about
in the billowing sheet. But her feet
are bound to the blashy ground,

and her hands bent on pummelling
move fast, as the wind dries the sheet.
The thoughts of the woman
are big-bellied with child and bread

like the sheet in the buffeting wind:
she'll have the sheet pegged and dried
in the wind before the soot darkens it;
then she'll pummel the bread for the child.

I'm pegging my thoughts on the line
in the buffeting wind. I'm the wind
billowing thoughts, and they're blown
about like the great white sheet.

I'm the child in the big-bellied woman.
My hands pummel her belly as she pegs
the sheet. I'm the yeast in the bread,
and the blashy ground at her feet.

So we rub along together, the woman,
the wind, and the child: forever bent
on beating the soot, and drying the sheet,
so the bread can be pummelled, and rise.

Rag and bone man

Clip-clop down Monkbridge Road: *clip-clop clip-clop*
go the mangy horse with the clackety cart
and the wizened man with his sleeves rolled up
crying 'Raag Booan, Raag Booan. *Any ol' iron?*'
Then louder: *clippety-clop, clippety-clop*
the cart clatters right, down the bumpety road,
past the pillar box and the corner shop,
and the children chanting a hopscotch song
(with a hop and a skip and a skip-jump-hop)
in the way of the cart as it creaks along;
past women giving the back yard a mop,
while they watch the man on his rickety cart
clopping nearer and nearer, *clippety-clop*,
past the house at the top, then '*Whooa!*' and stop.

The attic

Up here, both worlds are visible –
but only by moving
from one window to another.

Always a choice: either shadowy
tree spires climbing high
among grey stone houses,

or red brick chimneys
dropping in gradual steps
down serrated roofs.

Never both at the same time –
unless, by standing
in the empty middle of this room

(where everything is arranged
round grey linoleum edges),
it's just possible

to bring each into view,
and our lives tilting
across the join?

Even from this distance, I feel
the gravitational pull.

Wood Lane

Again in darkness gingerly
dawn puts a cat's paw forward,
padding into morning.

Sleep drifts through
wakefulness. Memory prints
untidy tracks over melting

patches of dream
like messages encrypted
in a forgotten tongue.

Voices stir, as words stir
on a page half written
and waiting, folded away:

'In the wall, under the trees,
a stone is missing. Fairy horses
are stabled here during the day.

When evening comes,
so do the fairies. No one has seen them –
but walk here quietly, and you may.'

Light shifts and sways in tall
horse chestnut trees, leaving soft
malleable transfers where the stable lay.

Footsteps echo under the high
walls. Houses cast long
move-less shadows in the lane.

Toad

Toad squats at the bottom
of the Hollies,
where the rhododendrons

are thickest, deepest,
and the terraced path falls away
into the gulley.

You have to tread carefully
on the slippy stones which lead down
to his dripping den.

Just when voices from above
begin to fade, and you can hear
the beck's dank trickle,

you enter a passage
which winds through granite rocks
into a fern-fringed hollow.

And there you find him.
Even from behind
there's no mistaking

his massive haunches,
set in the ground foursquare
and rising steeply:

hard flanks heaving,
slimy green and scaly,
grained with lichen.

A lopsided grin creases half the girth
of his neck and sinks in the bulk
of his warted body.

It's a fifteen-foot drop
from his stony eyes to the ground under
his huge webbed feet.

When he moves the whole valley
rumbles, and the land from Leeds to Otley
shudders when he leaps.

Omnibus

for Emma

By a gate at the end of the Hollies
an old stone bath stood still,
till we climbed aboard, and our fares
were paid, and we rang the bell.

Then we lifted off, and our magic bus
took us soaring high.
We waved, and the trees waved back at us
through the cloudy sky.

It was a ha'penny to Uganda
and a penny to Peru;
thrupence to Samarkand or Zanzibar,
a tanner to Timbuctoo.

Wherever took our fancy
we journeyed in our bus,
which by some wild necromancy
transported all of us.

We crossed the Red Sea from Cairo,
we roamed the desert sands.
We followed dad on his journey
across the hot poor lands.

We saw the naked children
beside the coffee trees,
and tiny huts built of murram
roofed with banana leaves.

A woman holding a pitcher
had a baby on her back.
Heat hazed the far horizon
and cracked the baked red track.

All aboard… we were up and away
to Mars or the yellow moon
and back safe in the Hollies
before you could say we'd gone.

August, and the hollyhocks

for Ann Squires

August, and the hollyhocks are reaching
all-time record heights. The tallest, a reckless
nine-foot spire of crimson saucers shooting
up, up, into an endless blue of sky, turns
at its topmost tip and droops like a spent rocket.

We are Lilliputians in a jungle of them,
rooted where they seeded haphazardly
among the crazy paving. Run wild,
they sprout *slowly* umbrella leaves,
their crumpled florets frail and veined as faces.

Straddling the jigsaw pieces, we practise
our biggest steps and reaches: stretching on tiptoe,
making our arms be pinnacles pointing skyward,
or opening them wide like arches.
We tilt our faces – platters in the sun; warmth

for golden pollen. Or we sway from side to side,
shedding crimson finery for pods of seed.
We are fabulous. Our worth in hollyhocks
is measured, not by frill and flounce, but stretch,
thickness of stem: vigour's spread and stride.

Snicket

for Gill and Kate

Darker than the ginnel
from home to town,
tunnelling between
tree-shadowy houses;

or from home
to Meanwood pond
through tight herringbone
streets and alleys

(carrying four nets
in assorted colours,
and four empty jam jars
on Saturdays);

narrower than the track
over woody parkland
to green frogspawn pond
and on to the Hollies,

taking the back way
among scratchy brambles
and smearing faces
with fat blackberries;

longer than all-the-way-
home, straggling
with the chatty beck
among nettles and dock-leaves

(carrying four nets
in assorted colours
and jam jars full of tadpoles
on Saturdays):

darker, narrower,
longer than all these
is the snicket
from then to now,

holding them
carefully
so as not to spill
them sideways.

The Misses Hallewell

Today they take their constitutional:
one in lilac, one in green, as usual.

Their patio is dense with hollyhocks.
Butterflies flit among the buddleias

or settle on the tall white scented phlox.
Bumble bees hum in the lavender;

a wood-pigeon is churr-churr-
churring from a nearby rooftop,

and somewhere at the back
an ice cream van plays 'Clementine',

its tinny tinkle chiming
with their steady summer almanac.

Last to read

'No stopping you now.' The teacher
smiled, and gave me thrupence –
my prize for being the last to read.
I slipped it in my pocket,
feeling my worth grow.

All the way home, road signs
blazoned prohibitions: *No Parking,
No Entry, No Waiting*. Adverts, clear
as wet newsprint, started from bill boards,
their letters all pertly prinked.

The familiar world became a moving
transcript of itself, with gaps between
the words where things had been,
like space turning solid or a linocut
with the hollow patches inked.

Nearing Headingley, the map settled.
Street names seemed newly stamped
with the certainty of being understood:
Shaw Lane, Monkbridge Road, Brookfield Road.
Houses stood still and unchanged.

All the same, I held my treasure tight
for fear the words might unravel,
the syllables come undone,
and all the alphabet come tumbling down
like beads off a broken string.

Transposed

for Geoffrey Hartman

And there, with fingers interwoven, both hands
Pressed closely, palm to palm, and to his mouth
Uplifted, he, as through an instrument,
Blew mimic hootings to the silent owls
That they might answer him.
                                    Wordsworth, *The Prelude*

Nothing so eerie as this ululating,
low, orbicular 'To... whoo'. A magic
trick performed by the initiate with two
cupped hands and breath. A sound as slow
and round as a glass bubble blown, which
grows as long as the glass-blower blows,
and hangs suspended when the blowing stops.
A skill withheld, or painstakingly acquired
through dull apprenticeship. Then suddenly

a sound. And with the sound, the exact spot
in which the sound first came, and stopped.

There: I am standing by Meanwood pond,
as the boy stood by the lake of Winander.
My cupped hands are a vessel of sound
which carries over the limpid pond, just as
my body continues, transposed in still water.
While in the sound *I* am no longer *me*,
but nor is the sound either owl or child.
I am shadowy, crepuscular: I blow
for the sound's sake, its lone
witchery. Expecting no answer.

Saturday afternoon on the Ridge

The wind is up – raking beeches,
stirring low among alder branches,
and bending the spindly trunks of birches.
Clearings are islands of traffic sound

blown up from the long grey
trailing ribbon of Meanwood Road.
That disused bandstand is bleak
and marooned as a winter pier.

Out here, where the trees end,
wind buffets the sledge-slope,
thwacks the broad flat face
of Ridge terrace like a cliff.

High over house-tops,
gulls tumble and cry – circling,
circling in the empty air.
Here all the ginnels come to a stop.

Land falls away. Sugarwell
is folded in distant greenness,
and Meanwood has been
far out at sea all day.

Trading conkers

All night, rooks called in the beating wind,
wind rocked in the long arms of trees, rain
pelted the big hands of horse-chestnut leaves,
leaves weltered down. Along Grove Lane
and Shire Oak Road, the heavy conkers fell.

In the morning, under tousled trees,
Headingley lay strewn with sodden leaves.
Safe and unblemished in their green pronged
shells, half-hidden conkers gleamed
a dark, rich, molten chocolate brown.

We carried them away in basket loads –
backs bowed by the weight of plunder.
Proudly we bore them home like treasure
and sorted them in shining rows for trade
by size and colour, hardness, texture.

Later, on a jaunt to Oxford, mum returned
with a carload of conkers. Mounds
of them, an unfamiliar flecked ochre,
spilled on the carpet, shining. We ogled
them like Silas Marner, counting.

In grades of excellence on window sills
they dulled to a matt monochrome,
shrivelled into bitter nut-hard nuggets
and gathered dust in cardboard boxes.
Now, I'd trade them all in

with the quads, the spires, the Cotswold stone
for rooks calling in the high wind,
wind rocking in the tall trees
and all along the roads in Headingley
the muffled thud of conkers falling.

Brambling

Mouths bloodied purple, fingers antennae
trembling for touch of hidden fruit –

foragers scouring the hinterland,
eyes skinned for dark swell of berry.

Our days are long, and battle-scarred
with brambling. Brummels lade our nights;

all our tomorrows are a hooked tunnel
of *bummelkites*. We move hungrily

among edges, hunting for certainties:
scavengers off a darkened street,

hardened hierophants
in the sacred lore of blackberries.

We love beck-sides, and all derelict places
where branches scramble out of sight –

behind nettles, under hawthorns, sidling
through bracken. We are long-armed

with reaching for the woody stems
that clamber at an immense height.

But most of all we love the brambles
arching spindly over walls in ginnels –

stray offerings from untidy ends of gardens,
bending with plump black weight.

Landscape near Otley

Wind on high edgeless fells,
and sheep like knobbly stones
scattered thin under long walls.
Sky a single unbroken plane of grey,
with nothing as far as the eye can see
but promise of heather –
miles and miles of dark purply-brown,
massed in low tumps under swelling hills.

Not even Cotman would try
a palette so muted, a canvas so empty.

All but the drabbest pigment drained away,
and nothing to break the three matt bands
of purply-brown, grey-green, and grey,
but a few pale dabs for the sheep
under the thin, wandering, diagonal
belt of drystone wall,
where the threadbare grain of high fells
meets the flat grey wash of sky.

Walls

for the Metcalfes of Appersett

I love the curt sounds of the vowels –
the way they hold back and stay put
like through-stones in wind-bitten walls:
'appen, mucky, luv, thissen, mek, nowt.
The consonants sturdy as footings
or knobbly as topstones, with a shut
sound – *taffled, snicket, sneck, tekken* –
to keep the sheep in and the gales out.
All the words rough and showing
their edges, with glottal stops as packers:
Ah s'll be dahn on mi nogs ower lang
bah missen in t' claggy muck and watter.
And the whole fabric holding together
without mortar against age and weather.

Ginneling

for Jenny Harrison

Ginnle *v. Also ginle, ginnel. To tickle (the gills of a fish): to tickle (trout), catch by tickling the gills, etc.*

Oxford English Dictionary

Holding still. Stretched flat
on bevelled stone, head down –
hushed, level with edge –

hearing the smooth steady
lap lap lapping below dark pool ledge.
Underwater arm trawling

the deep cold shelving greeny black,
reaching back, and further
for oily touch of scaly skin on skin.

Skilled fingers quiver
round sleek slither
belly of quicksilver.

Sudden flicker-flurry at the catch.
Writhing taut in flexed grip,
grounded gasping on dry shelf –

a swift thudding blow: exact.
Heavy, stunned, limp,
jaw gaping, jowl cracked,

sideways on, sheen dulling,
top of the pile in a bucket, flat-packed.
One chill goggle eye staring.

Juan taught me

what to do with chewing gum,
where to go for gob-stoppers,
how to unclog a sherbet fountain,
which tree had the best conkers;

how the street's camber steers
a marble, when to treble load a cap-gun,
how broken glass can start a fire,
the exact angle for ignition;

the non-existence of Father Christmas,
how to knot a conker string,
when I should mind my own business,
why nettles don't always sting;

the short cuts at the back of Bentley
Lane and Meanwood, why it was odd
not to live with my granny,
go to church, or believe in God;

the way to coax grubs into a jam jar,
whether to pickle, drown, or grill them;
how to adorn cement and molten tar,
leaving my initials in them;

how to catch a louse and crack
its carapace, short vowels and the F-word,
how to spin a stone along the beck
and aim an air-gun at a blackbird;

what old tyres are for, making
a bike rear on its hind wheel,
taking angles, sudden breaking,
how to smoke and hide the smell;

to wish I was a boy and working class;
not how to thank him, or bring back his face.

Playin' out

'*Yer playin' out?*' and off we'd go:
coats, hats, *incognito,*

wearing our back-street voices
as shades or disguises.

Old words revived each day
as if we'd never been away:

riled for angry, *mash* for tea,
cop it, courtin', aye.

New ones sank straight in
as if they'd always been,

or settled gradually:
mazzled, mawngy, gradely.

Every day softened the transition
between us and them.

But still the big house and garden:
the not quite forgiven or forgotten;

the gaps, the embarrassing
thresholds, the voices slipping.

Meanwood ginnel

We're going places.

Barbed wire like steely brambles
lines the ditches,
long and deep as trenches,
between this rambling uncertain ginnel
and the small back garden sheds
of red brick houses.

No one about.
We're kicking over the traces.

Here, on a scrap of earth
between mill-dump and pig-pen
the ginnel ends in open path
then peters out in grit and gravel.
The tannery watches
with a hundred sunken eyes
over the low slumped sacks of fleeces.

Nothing doing.
We're marking time

as makeshift fences
(corrugated iron, chipboard,
chicken wire, wooden planks)
mark out the tatty edges
of this no man's land
we have in common –

going nowhere and dawdling in,
with truant faces.

Pig-pen at Meanwood

A stone's throw from the tannery
a row of small allotments lay,
flat under the sun in squares

like drying laundry. The air
stank of seared hide, flowering
currant, manure, and chemicals.

Soil, a finely furrowed brown,
was thickly sewn in clumps and frills
with greens. Lettuces plumped;

beans tendrilled; dandelions
and dock-leaves in scratty patches
roughly fringed the edges.

Huddling behind a ragged screen
of foxgloves, willow-herb and nettles
sat the long, low, red brick pig-pen.

Mounds of pink gruntlings
grubbed in the swill or nuzzled the sows'
dugs: six at a time, and wriggling.

Sunlight on chicken wire at noon
printed regular grey diamonds
like stitching on quilts and eiderdowns

all over the fleshy flanks of pigs,
who swayed heavily from side to side
like great moving beds

or heaved clean and quivering in the mud,
stacked one against the other, sated –
row on row of hides.

Mill Pond dump

Tannery's spew. Huge breathing beast's
sloughed-off integument, encrusted

with time's leavings – orts, scraps, relics;
treasures and trinculos, unsorted through.

Intricate things are best, with cogs and springs;
these can be retrieved with sticks.

Once I hooked out an old stopwatch, thick
as my fist, the insides rusting: my best find.

I could take it apart, wind and unwind
the dial, feel the serrated wheels turning.

The glass was missing, but the hinged
face was still intact – with a catch that clicked.

Hidden in my pocket I can feel it, ticking.

Bandstand

On our crinkly, yellowing, Sellotaped-up map,
a small rectangle marked 'Works'
sits just under Sugarwell Hill Park,
an inch from Meanwood Valley Urban Farm.

Seen from the Ridge, it's a Lowry picture:
the long, angular, red brick building
below a flat-topped slag-heap kind of hill
with the usual tiny matchstick men

going to and fro past dark doorways
on a road that's straight, perfectly level,
bearing the dreary no-hope feeling of it all
under a sagging, squared-off sky.

Up here, it's spring in Batty's wood –
snowdrops over, daffodils stirring
like a bright fringe under a dark coat,
bark on flickering branches a soft green.

That bandstand has seen better days.
A hundred years ago, on spring bank holidays,
a jaunty band would sit there, striking up a tune,
and all the little Lowry matchstick men

would promenade above the town
with wives or sweethearts on their arms,
and pause to contemplate the nearby scene
while music drifted lightly, debonairly, down.

Thornton's Arcade

The Arcade beckons like Blackpool Pier.
Shop windows spangle: booths at a fair.
Signs swing high on wrought iron brackets,
creaking, squeaking and making a racket.
Crowds hurry in from the rain on Briggate,
loaded down with food from the market.
A gaggle of kids gathers under the clock
to watch the big hand with its slow *tick tock*.
Older ones shuffle. Younger ones stare
at the *tableau vivant* standing up there,
glossy and kitsch in the cold morning air.

It's Robin Hood with his horn and a bow,
and Gurth the swineherd from *Ivanhoe*,
in bright green tunic and yellow hair,
and Richard the Lionheart home from the war,
and Friar Tuck in his short brown frock.
They all stand ready, over the clock,
to bang the bells at the quarter hour,
displaying their shiny pink musculature;
and we're braced for the sound
as the hand creeps round.

Ding dong, ding dong, they ring all the day long
till the time when the gold which the rich people store
will be loaded in sacks and returned to the poor,
from Sherwood Forest to Woodhouse Moor.

Bryan's Fish Shop

Women in overalls with shiny red faces
have sliced the potatoes in thick white wedges.
They've gutted and filleted the big cod,
banking them in slabs on clean tiled ledges,
and now they dunk them in smooth grey batter
then lower them over the deep vat's edges.
The shop fugs up with steam and chatter.
Their hands move fast as they take their orders,
raising and lowering, filling and emptying
their metal basket, meshed like a net,
in time with the ebb and flow of customers.

'*Cod 'n' chips please, wi' salt 'n vinegar.*'

The cod are left in a hot sea, sizzling,
to be hauled in crispy golden and wet
from the scalding spit and spatter of fat.
Then they're wrapped in a wad of *Yorkshire Post*
and carried away from the bustle and hiss.
More hygienic in plastic trays, but best
eaten hot off the press, like this.

Mr Bradshaw

'*Tac-i-turn*' I repeated, tri-syllabically –
turning my new word like a key.
His shop was no deeper than our kitchen,
but climbed sheer as a rock face on the Chevin,
every dark inch of edge hooked and hung
with huge dusty extension cables, which swung
heavily in coils over ridges, fissures, cavities.
Wires, plugs, adaptors, flexes, fuses
crammed the cracks and crusted the crevices.
His fist was a hammer pounding an anvil,
his clutch a vice. He had fingers tough as bradawls
for fixing things. His blue overalls smelt of oil,
sweat, burnt metal; and his eyes were black holes
sunk in sockets, looking a long way in.

He was forever gruff, or silent. When I last saw him,
he was mending our kettle in silence, drinking his tea.
Back in Leeds recently, passing that way,
I saw the shop front boarded up behind graffiti:
thirty unspoken years like secrets sealed in.
What was that word again? *Taciturn*, the old key.

Prosaic

*All day I could hear the clanging of trams and at night the shunting of
trains from the nearby marshalling yards, and in the small hours the parish
church clock chiming, and in the morning the clatter of horses' hooves, the
rumble of wagons and lorries, the distant street cries from the Market, the
droning trams again, the factory hooters, the clanking of brewers' drays
delivering their crates and barrels, the small thunder of cattle on their way
to the slaughterhouse, the revving-up of buses, the shouts of the news-
vendors, the voices of work-mates exchanging banter, the bolting back of
doors, the whistling of porters and errand boys, the rat-a-tat of postmen,
the far-off tinkling of the arcade carillons...*
Keith Waterhouse, City Lights, 1994

See how this shopping-list of movables
branches and multiplies as it grows
thicker, more voluble, into a veritable
cornucopia of urban noise that flows
and overflows, its long *et cetera* of audibles
gathering texture as it speeds or slows
to catch the city's unending variables
and lay them out in tactile rows
like piles of fruit and vegetables –
or toss them, as a fishmonger throws
gleaming fish in heaps on market-stalls.
How well this bustling inventory in prose
serves memory's complex multiples.

Comfortable box

Nothing so cheerfully compact
as the full fat cardboard box
delivered Fridays, proudly stacked
by our man from Groocock's.

All the groceries in reassuring
rows and labelled layers,
their clean edges touching
flush, like days on calendars.

Every packet, carton, tin and jar
pronouncing regularity and order:
frugal plenty parcelled out, as far
as Friday next, or further –

like months of earnings
laid end to end to end;
or rationed treats and savings
paid their final dividend.

Plain as the lettering
on squares sitting side by side,
all our comings and goings
are here centred, simplified.

I can no more remember Friday
without this comfortable box
than home without Headingley
or childhood without Groocock's.

Across the street

Juan's mum carries in
her Co-op shopping
just as the Groocock's van
is pulling up and stopping.
I wave as I hurry in,
leaving the back gate open.

Open. The day's shadows
have moved across the street.
I wonder if we'll be playing out.
I can hear the latch on her gate
clicking as she swings it shut.

Truant

School slumps over its own
slack shadow, half asleep in the sun –
its stony vigilance gone

with the tidying of classrooms,
closing of windows, fading
of voices, locking of doors.

Not a sound, not a movement
in the dusty yard, where time
has been busy all these years

shrinking the empty stretch
between gateway and doorway
to its meagre span.

Why, then, as I stand
at the dwindled railings, looking in,
am I the guilty child all over again –

time suddenly given back to me,
made strangely my own,
like holidays lasting all the summer long?

Map

The streets at the back are wandering seams —
threads I can pull, or unravel and run —

but the long straight road at the front
is a smooth unbreakable hem.

Dad comes and goes down a thin corridor
that cuts through the Ridge to Woodhouse Moor.

He moves with quick steps, quietly,
carrying an old brown briefcase and a key.

Absences

A hard spin could turn
the blue globe round,
fast and furious as the big wheel –
but never fast or furious
or round enough for us,
during his absences.

All the long days naughty,
expectant, fatherless.
Stamps stuck on postcards
like empty promises:
flash-back images,
raw as usurped memories.

Uganda, home of origins
lost on the runway,
like the crowd of farewell faces
dwindling through the years
to mirages, or slipping
in and out of dreams.

And only dad unchanged,
returning with wooden crocodiles
or hand-painted beads –
still small and definite
among the deepening
grey shades of Leeds.

Eleven-plus

With the last of the summer days,
the terrace shrank to half its size.
Familiar things looked strange,
even to themselves.

Leeds elongated between schools.
Ginnels hid behind bus routes
in and out of the wide city.
Streets lost detail, texture –
like a finished tapestry
with the knobbly ends
of threads tucked out of sight,
as though unfit for public view.

With the last of the summer days
came altered passwords,
new allegiances.

We moved uneasily
on hidden thresholds:
speaking slowly, pausing to explain,
as if our words could be translated
back into themselves again.

Penny for the guy

No history of November keeps the guy
Ivor Gurney

Bloat belly beggar:
back propped, stick legs buckled,
head heavy like a goitred pumpkin,
lolling. Two pleading stumps
for arms.

Yesterday we tossed pennies
into his Yorkshireman's cloth cap.
Today we burn him:
inch by inch,
treachery for treachery.

Even now, I see his crooked shape
lit up like a neon scarecrow
under a throbbing sky:
treason's simulacrum,
his charred face real enough.

Alibi, 22 November 1963

We all know where we were when it happened:
our actions in sequence like a dream,
and the scene playing back again in slow motion.

Shadows in the street and children among fallen
leaves, the garden gate left open:
we all know where we were when it happened.

Coming in from the garden, no one in the kitchen
and the hall silent like a premonition,
and the scene playing back again in slow motion.

Finding you ironing by the television.
A sudden shot, then a repetition.
We all know where we were when it happened.

You standing in front of the screen, to soften
the shock and prevent the intrusion
and the scene playing back again in slow motion.

The crowd stilled under the Dallas sun.
Loudspeakers, the motorcade in confusion:
we all know where we were when it happened.

An instant for the assassination
and the world changed in slow motion
like a dream and the scene playing back again
to when it happened and we all knew where we were.

Alma Road

i.m. Jacqueline Hill,
murdered by the Yorkshire Ripper,
17 November 1980

What did I expect, after all these years
(and me nowhere near home
since it happened)?

The site still cordoned off,
a forensic ring marking the spot
where her cream-coloured, blood-

spattered raffia handbag fell,
then (a few yards away) her Fair Isle
knitted mitten, her spectacles?

A chalk silhouette, perhaps,
or a plaque: *Twenty years old.*
His thirteenth and final victim.

How high the nettles grow
against the wall, under the tree.
How casually the passers-by pass by.

Cleo's songs

'My bonnie lies over the ocean,
My bonnie lies over the sea…'

She stretched the coverlet so tight
the mattress bent like a hull
and held us rocking, rocking,
to her sad low voice in the song.

'In the deep mid-winter
Frosty wind made moan…'

Darkness swayed to her words
as sky in the heavy trees
swayed on the high white Ridge
where sledges climbed and fell.

'Pack up your troubles in your old kit bag
And smile smile smile…'

From Headingley to Sugarwell
the ginnels snaked in tiny hairline saps.
We sang as we marched in single file,
smashing the ice on the puddle tops.

'It's a long way to Tipperary,
It's a long way to go…'

Her voice in the song lingered on, like a cry,
for her married name on a distant stone,
and all the lines of nameless graves
across the sodden fields of Picardy.

Town Hall lions

Methinks I see in my mind a noble and puissant Nation rousing herself like a strong man after sleep, and shaking her invincible locks

Milton, *Areopagitica*

Old friends lying prone
under huge columns of stone,
I remember you

steep and black as the night,
with cavernous nostrils
and swishing manes;

not pale and crumbling
and spattered –
dozing, apathetic,

as municipal Leeds traipses by
on the Headrow – your only
contribution a desultory

'No War on Iraq'
felt-tipped on one flank
under a pigeon dropping.

Time to wake up, old friends.
You've been there
for too long without moving.

Baking

Strange, her knack for turning up
these thirty-odd years
when I least expect her:

ironing, folding the sheets,
or most often baking cakes;
so that I stop to consider

how, involuntarily,
sounds, thoughts, smells, shapes
are habits arranged round her face.

Suddenly, through a half-open
window, comes warm layered scent
of syringa, bonfires, mown grass.

How readily the present folds away:
everything standing back
from itself, unchanged –

the terrace from the road,
the house a long way off down the garden,
rooms deepening through the hall,

light falling in its usual place
by the kitchen window
where she stands, baking cakes.

Someone down the terrace
is mowing their lawn, and our side
of the street is in cool quiet shadow.

Front to back, home lengthens,
making what is familiar
past, particular, necessary, strange.

Grove Lane in September

He's been bending for so long
over his bonfire, feeding it with leaves,
that he stoops like an old man:

eyes smarting from the smoke,
face wrinkled like a walnut
by the dry heat of the blaze,

or browned more slowly like a berry
in the steady warmth of the sun.
He's been there for hours

working on that scrubby bit of earth
by the gate in the grey stone wall
at the end of the narrow garden.

(Leaning on your long rake,
you listen to the quick insistent crackle
and spit of the rust-coloured leaves,

hearing the sound of children
and the intermittent hum
of Sunday traffic on its slow way home.)

It's early evening still,
and with his head tilted slightly
to one side he looks far away –

like someone who has been standing there
so long, tending his fire and thinking,
he has become an old man.

Homesickness

Codham, Cockridden, Childerditch,
Roses, Pyrgo and Lapwater,
I shall give them all to my elder daughter.
        Edward Thomas, 'If I should ever grow rich'

Nothing like place-names for the narrow miss,
calling down the avenue of years
for lost originals.

No wonder Thomas loved them,
holding them close
and chanting them like a spell

to keep the darkness still –
every syllable aching
for the one thing unconditional.

And you, dad, what would you give me?
Otley, Ilkley, Armley,
Roundhay, Meanwood, Headingley:

lullabies lacing the night,
or stepping stones beyond –
each one edging a little closer home?

At the back

In Oakfield Terrace as the light ebbs
and children's shouts grow faint,

streets empty, cats stir in the shadows,
milk-bottles are set out on steps.

The days are drawing in. A wireless
somewhere is playing 'Penny Lane'.

It's back-endish. There's a nip in the air.
Tomorrow, school starts up again.

Hide and Seek

No garden appears, no path, no hoar-green bush
Of Lad's-love, or Old Man, no child beside,
Neither father nor mother, nor any playmate;
Only an avenue, dark, nameless, without end.
               Edward Thomas, 'Old Man'

Along this stretch of muddy pathway
breasting the Hollies
all's stilled to a hush under dripping trees.
Sun gleams on the flat green oily laurel leaves.

Ivy, bracken, rhododendron,
have long since buried
our stone bath in oblivion,
but the hollow made when there was a river
is a great bin of ferns and stones going on for ever,
where a child can hide.

My eyes are shut behind tight fingers,
and I am counting slowly:
eighteen, nineteen, twenty...
'Coming, ready or not!'

Ready or not,
I'm a long way off
like a dream
and my voice in the dream
making no sound.

I call and call down the pathway
to the hollow
through cupped hands.

The bend

for Mike, in memory of Sally

As we filed down the ginnel, turned the bend
and broke into a run
we knew who'd be first to reach the end.

Every Sunday the same: mum would send
us out in the morning sun.
As we filed down the ginnel and turned the bend

you were laughing. I could touch your hand
as you broke into a run.
We knew who'd be first to reach the end.

I was always there with you, one step behind
your shadow in the sun
as we filed down the ginnel and turned the bend,

your laughter carried away by the wind
as you broke into a run.
We knew you'd be first to reach the end
as we filed down the ginnel, and turned the bend.

Riddle

I have known you all my life
but you were always a riddle.

Open or closed,
discontinuous and criss-crossed,

you carry me everywhere
and back again.

You are labyrinthine,
have no endings or beginnings.

Cunning as a fish
and hard as stones

you snag me as I catch you
slipping away.

Crossing the Ridge

The longest ginnel I know
moves across the map
like two big tacking-stitches
or the broken furrow of a plough.

It starts where the bluebells grow
under the oaks in Batty's wood
and climbs in a deep groove
between tall houses, over the brow

of the Ridge to the far side,
where it blanks out
on Cumberland Road in brightness:
empty, un-selving, wide.

Then it rallies; and down –
diagonally left and down –
it delves like something
dark and purposive, into town.

Thirty years since I walked here,
and not a stone changed.
Only a moment's hesitation
after climbing, as I stand where

the ginnel closes on light
and opens on darkness –
caught in the bright hiatus,
a thief in the night.

Notes

'Toad': the Hollies is a wooded park to the west of Leeds, about twenty minutes from Headingley.

'Snicket': like 'ginnel', a Yorkshire dialect word for passageway, especially when this is a short-cut.

'Brambling': 'brummel' and 'bummelkite' (bumblekite) are Yorkshire dialect words for blackberry, but less common than 'bramble'.

'Landscape near Otley': John Sell Cotman was an eighteenth-century watercolourist, celebrated for his paintings of Yorkshire and Lake District scenes. Many of his paintings are housed in Leeds City Art Gallery.

'Walls': 'appen': maybe; 'thissen': you; 'mek': make; 'nowt': nothing; 'taffled': tangled; down on my knees for too long in the sticky mud and water.

'Mr Bradshaw': the Chevin is a steep rocky ridge on the road from Leeds to Otley.

'Absences': I was born in Uganda, and we returned there for two years, 1964–6.

'Penny for the Guy': Guy Fawkes was from York. The custom of burning effigies of him on 5 November was upheld with particular enthusiasm in Yorkshire.

'Alibi, 22 November 1963': the date of John F. Kennedy's death.

'Town Hall lions': twenty years or so ago, the centre of Leeds was cleaned up. Buildings that once were pitch black are now strangely blanched.